Thousands of Years of Prayers

Thousands of Years of Prayers

poems by

Julie Dunlop

SHANTI ARTS PUBLISHING
BRUNSWICK, MAINE

Thousands of Years of Prayers

Published by Shanti Arts Publishing
Designed by Shanti Arts Designs

Cover image and interior photographs by Julie Dunlop and used with her permission.

Shanti Arts LLC
193 Hillside Road
Brunswick, Maine 04011

shantiarts.com

Printed in the United States of America

ISBN: 978-1-956056-68-6 (softcover)

Library of Congress Control Number: 2022952191

Dedicated with gratitude, respect, and love
to River *Gaṅgā*
and
to India
past, present, and future

Contents

A Mix of Saffron and Charred Ash ... 11
Unlocking Time and Space ... 12
Sweetening the Ordinary Mums ... 14
Currents Shifting Already ... 16
Blooming into Strange Beauty ... 17
River of Prayer ... 18
Small Orbs of Light ... 20
Illuminating the Flames ... 21
Floating on Your Currents ... 22
Infinite and Infinitesimal ... 23
Your Heartsong ... 24
The Same Sky ... 25
Meditative Flow ... 26
Surrendering to the Flow ... 27
Is There Anywhere You Are Not? ... 28
Before the World Awakes ... 30
The Swirl of It All ... 32
Collective Ocean of Consciousness ... 34
Feeding Upon the Light of Stars ... 35
Unwinding Our Knots ... 36
One Dissolving Particle at a Time ... 37
Out of the Muddiest of Waters ... 38
Your Abiding Waters ... 40
Coming Together Like Two Hands in Prayer ... 42
That Space Within ... 44
Beyond What Can Be Measured ... 46
Always Present, Always Flowing ... 48
Accepting Every Leg, Every Arm ... 49
Until We Stop and Pause ... 50
Each Exhale Taking Us Closer ... 52
Resonance Eight Centuries Later ... 54
You Are ... 56
All of This and More ... 58
Universal Flow ... 60

The Singer and the Song 62
Anchor of the Years 63
Breathing into the Space of Not Knowing 64
Struggles Fading Away 66
River of Resonance 68
Are We Not All a River 69
Counterbalancing 70
The Flow of Awareness 72
You Bathe Us 74
Moving Beyond the Body 78
Reawakening 80
Into the Sacred Spaces 82
Moving Beyond Language 84
With Each Breath 86
Thousands of Years of Prayers 88
Undeniable *Saṃskāras* 90
In the Quiet Knocking of Boats 92
To the Heavens 94
Carrying Away Fear 96
Sacred Bridge 98
Beckoning Me to Stay 100
Into Your Waters 101
Nourished by Your Waters 102
Beyond Reach 104
Appearing Like Magic 106
Our Invincibility Dissolving 108
By Your Waters 110
Lifesong 112
Storm-Laden Lungs 114
Like a Boat Not Yet Seen 115
An Inexplicable Resonance 116
Blooming Unseen 118
Awakening the Stars 120
When Your Waters Braid 122
Flowing Like a Chant Without End 124
A Million Tiny Circles Expanding 126
Wellsprings of Peace 127
Your Holy *Jal* 128

A Mix of Saffron and Charred Ash

Dear *Gaṅgā*,

Even here in the desert
of the American Southwest,
I hear your call—
a mix of saffron
and charred ash,

the songs of the *ghāṭs*[1]
keeping me awake tonight

Sunrise there has already come
and gone, spreading
across your currents
its golden light

1. *ghāṭ* (from *ghaṭṭa*): steps leading down to a river

Unlocking Time and Space

Dear *Gaṅgā*,

In the shimmering
of your waters,
you hear me,

with your mystical ways
of knowing, unlocking time
and space,
the thousands of miles
between us
dissolving

until you are flowing
right by my sofa
continents away,

the choir of the spirits
you've carried home
still resonant—
Shāntiḥ Shāntiḥ Shāntiḥ[1]

your peace expanding
inexplicably,
immeasurably,

1. *Shāntiḥ Shāntiḥ Shāntiḥ:* Peace, Peace, Peace

in widening circles
rippling out
into
the
community,
out
into
the
world

Sweetening the Ordinary Mums

Dear *Gaṅgā*,

Even while my feet
are still planted
in the desert soil
so far from you,

you are sweetening
the ordinary mums
lined up
at the grocery store
until they shimmer,

you are awakening
the rippled texture
of the couch,
the spice
of pumpkin muffins,
the scent
of late-blooming roses,
the sounds
of voices I hear each day

you're washing my eyes clean
to see scuffed slippers anew
suddenly precious
as if sewn with gold,

and a sixteen-year-old car, paint peeling,
becoming a chariot as regal as they come

You have transported me,
returned me,
and renewed me
even before passport's
first stamp

Currents Shifting Already

Dear *Gaṅgā*,

I am being emptied out
one cupboard at a time,
one expectation at a time,

even the mailbox emptying
as mail forwards already
to another address,
my physical body still residing
at my ordinary address,
my astral body somewhere
between here
and your riverbanks,

all that is known to me
about to be emptied out
as the tides of Indian sounds,
sights, and scents rush
toward me,

my currents shifting already
as departure date draws near,
as if my molecules
are beginning
to move
in a choreography
of translation
in a realm
far beyond
logic's
reach

Blooming into Strange Beauty

Dear *Gaṅgā*,

How many millions of eyes
have gazed at you—
thousands of years
flowing together,
your sacred *nāḍīs*[1]
like a magnet drawing millions
longing to see your fires lit,
the flower petal offerings
drifting by,
the procession of death
blooming into strange beauty,

immersed in the *līlā*[2]
of coming and going,
rivers of tears
washing the faces
of mourners and seekers,
tourists and *sādhus*[3],

realizations coming to light
in the embrace of space,

shedding like a snake's skin
the debris

1. *nāḍī:* subtle energy pathways in the body
2. *līlā:* divine play or dance
3. *sādhu:* holy person

River of Prayer

Dear *Gaṅgā*,

River of imagination,
river of prayer so real
in the hearts of *sādhus*[1]
sitting by your side chanting—
the *stotras*[2] and *ślokas*[3] flowing
into your currents
for generations

Oh *Gaṅgā*,
what shapes do the boats trace
across your waters...

and what does the choreography
of their molecules reveal?

How do the flickers of light
from the floating candles feel
as they glimmer on your waters?

The sunlight and moonlight
translating their song
to all that swim
beneath your surface

1. *sādhu:* holy person
2. *stotra:* hymn of praise
3. *śloka:* poetic verse in Sanskrit

Thousands of years
of *ārati*[1] chants
at dawn and dusk
woven into your waters,

their vibrations
resonating
across time
and space

1. *ārati (ārātrika, ārti):* ceremonial offering of light to a deity

Small Orbs of Light

Dear *Gaṅgā*,

I am holding on to you
even as you slip through my hands

Who am I to hold a river?

Who am I to know
where this begins
and ends?
A flow beyond logic
tumbling through me
like some uncharted storm
detectable only to my nerves
digesting this all in strange dreams,
in uneven sleep, in an unsteady
countdown of days
until I take flight

Birds threading over you
with their songs
born from delicate throats
glowing like jewels,
like gems,
like sacred small orbs
of light

Illuminating the Flames

Dear *Gaṅgā*,

Watching full lives reduced to ash,
a steady stream of death,
family and friends bereft,
the light of *diyas*[1]
reflecting on your surface

You, the open-eyed witness,
emboldening us to look
unflinchingly at skulls
illuminating the flames,
the loves of our lives
going up in smoke,

and yet who can stop
the flood of gold at sunrise,
the symphony of saffron and turmeric
and *kumkum*[2]
filling the sky
as the sun sets over every cemetery,
every crematorium
every unmarked grave of loss?

---

1. *diya:* a small ghee candle, many of which float on the *Gaṅgā*
2. *kuṅkuma (kumkum):* a red sacred powder used for religious purposes

Floating on Your Currents

Dear *Gaṅgā*,

Lying on my back on the ground
I soften until I am floating
on your currents,
thousands of years
drifting beneath,
the bright blue sky above,

the day becoming night—
the sky full of stars,

the moon's luminous eye
gazing out
over our petty concerns
with compassion, as we float
or thrash,
churning as much or as little drama
as we choose,

going with the current
or against it,
the edges of the exhalation
and inhalation
meeting
as we surrender

into the rhythm
of the breath,
as we become one
with the gentle ease
of its flow

Infinite and Infinitesimal

Dear *Gaṅgā*,

We draw the light of the stars
into our fingertips

The water
of you, the oceans
and lakes
swimming
in our tears

Our collarbones, our shoulder blades,
our ribs, femurs
made of earth

Within the fire of our mind,
ideas, questions crackling

Through our nostrils, down our throat,
and into our bronchial wings
air gently flowing—

And the space—
the space between
two breaths—

is the space

between you
and me—

infinite
and
infinitesimal

Your Heartsong

Dear *Gaṅgā*,

At the international flight gate at Newark
a two-hour delay, mass confusion,

crowded in the heat, lines
snaking in every direction,

tributaries accumulating,
overflowing like a swollen river

And in the midst of it all
a golden body of light . . .
strangers, travelers fluent in this route
making this journey once a year—

like the sun, they brighten the path
guiding me into the enormous plane
hovering for fifteen hours—

Nova Scotia, the Atlantic Ocean,
the Caspian Sea, the Aegean Sea,
Tashkent, Kabul,
7000 miles later . . .
Mumbai!

Your heartsong awaiting,
Mā Gaṅgā[1],
25,005 feet
below

1. *Mā Gaṅgā:* the goddess of the Ganges, reverential name for River *Gaṅgā*

The Same Sky

Dear *Gaṅgā*,

I see you—your face
reflected in a thousand faces
on motorbikes, in rickshaws, on paths,
the streets alive, swarming with your music, your magic,
the symphony of horns,
hundreds of near-misses, the currents
shifting at just the right moment, death averted—

strange mixing of posh hotels and dilapidated shacks
making sense and nonsense—
the unpaved muddy areas, the bare feet,
Gaṇeśa[1] figurines perching on the dashboards,
the plaintive eyes of children begging
at the side of the car, bright pink flowers
cascading over torn-out buildings,
small monkeys in the hills beside the road,
a swirl of orange butterflies fluttering
through seven lanes of traffic and suddenly

we turn off the highway
into a quiet pocket of marigold garlands,
palm trees, coconut chutney, and twinkling lights,
the crescent of the moon hanging in the same sky
I pondered faraway, the same sky I flew through
to you, the same sky
that eyes have gazed at for millennia
changing and unchanging in the bruised brilliance
of each beleaguered day softly shuttling us
through the beauty to our graves

---

1. *Gaṇeśa:* elephant-headed deity known for removing obstacles

Meditative Flow

Dear *Gaṅgā*,

Appearing and disappearing,
the coming and going,
the real and unreal,
the *māyā*[1] of what is true and not true,
constantly in flux,
the crushed soul, the reviving sense of self,
the river of extremes
no match for your deep knowing

Can we recognize our *ātman*[2]
like a face reflected in the mirror
of your surface, your *jala*[3] transcending
the human mind, the human ego

Your currents constantly doing the laundry
of karma, *kurtas*[4],
bodies—both living and dead,
and consciousness, oscillating
between cloudy and clear,
the debris increasing
and decreasing as you,
survivor of so many lifetimes, continue
your
meditative
flow

1. *māyā:* illusion
2. *ātman:* soul
3. *jala:* water
4. *kurta:* loose collarless long shirt

Surrendering to the Flow

Dear *Gaṅgā*,

Compassionate one, you understand
the flow of energies within—
the terrain of *kāya*,[1]
the *srotas*[2] of bodily pathways,
the tributaries of blood and plasma
circulating inside the earth of our flesh,
the *nāḍīs*,[3] the subtle pathways
radiating from the navel,
carrying the *prāṇa* nourishing
the body, the spirit, the mind . . .

You, with your thousands of years' perspective,
understanding the flow of emotions,
the tides of worry, jealousy, frustration, sadness,
their rajasic,[4] tamasic[5] qualities
so different in texture
from the stream of consciousness
flowing purely, freely
in a quiet heart
that sees all and accepts all,
surrendering to the flow

---

1. *kāya:* the physical body
2. *srotas:* channels of circulation in the body
3. *nāḍī:* subtle energy pathways in the body
4. rajasic (from *rajasika*): referring to *rajas*, a quality of agitation, ambition, competition
5. tamasic (from *tamasika*): referring to *tamas*, a quality of sluggishness, depression

Is There Anywhere You Are Not?

Dear *Gaṅgā*,

In the pelting rain, the gentle rain,
the monsoon downpour, you are here

In the sounds of sirens and horns and train whistles,
bird calls and predawn chanting at temples nearby,
you are here

In the smoothness of *vaijayanti*[1] beads, the turning of the *mālā*[2],
bead by bead, *bīja*[3] mantra by *bīja* mantra,
you are here

In the smell of sandalwood attar, the thick texture of *bhākri*[4],
the sweetness of coconut chutney,
the *tikta rasa*[5] of bitter melon,
the sweetness of *chiku*[6] and custard apple,
you are here

In the purple flowers of the vines covering the walls
and the bright orange blooms on top of the high trees,
you are here

In the burning camphor of the *ārati*[7] at the altar
and in the sweet *prasād*[8] of dates,
you are here

---

1. *vaijayanti:* white sacred beads often connected in a *mālā* of 108 beads
2. *mālā:* a garland of meditation or prayer beads often used to keep count while chanting
3. *bīja:* seed sound, a one-syllable sacred sound, such as *Lam* for root chakra
4. *bhākri:* Indian-style bread made without wheat
5. *tikta rasa:* bitter taste
6. *chiku:* sapodilla/noseberry/mudapple
7. *ārati (ārātrika, ārti):* ceremonial offering of light to a deity
8. *prasāda (prasād):* a sweet offered during a ceremony

In the unpredictable flow of Wi-Fi in and out,
        the river of communication coming and going,
    you are here

I see you in the gold-painted horns of the cows
    and hear you in the ringing of the bells around their necks

Looking around:
        is there anywhere
    you are not?

Before the World Awakes

Dear *Gaṅgā*,

Illuminating us from afar,
sunrise upon your surface
shimmering in the molecules
of the mind,
the *brāhmamuhūrta*[1] sacred space
luminous inside

camphor, ghee,
dried cow dung,
and herbs
offered to the *kuṇḍa:*[2]
Sūryāya Svāhā
Sūryāya idaṃ na mama[3]

before the world awakes—
a blessed energy,
the transmutation of fire,
the *tilaka*[4] of turmeric and *kumkum,*[5]
the *vibhūti*[6] at the third eye,
wellspring of intuition
taking us beyond logic
beyond the mind
beyond everything

1. *brāhmamuhūrta:* sacred time before dawn, ideal for spiritual practice
2. *kuṇḍa:* a large copper container used in spiritual ceremony
3. *Sūryāya Svāḥ Sūryāya idaṃ na mama:* opening lines of the sunrise chant for *agnihotra*
4. *tilaka:* a mark of sacred herbal paste placed on the forehead
5. *kuṅkuma (kumkum):* red powder used on the forehead ceremonially
6. *vibhūti:* sacred ash

known and unknown—
purifying us
with practices
ancient
as the stars

The Swirl of It All

Dear *Gaṅgā*,

The women rolling incense sticks—
one by one into large bundles—
khus[1] mixing with *mitti*[2] with sandalwood
with rose with saffron—the colors,
aromas, textures merging—

the way scooters and trucks and cars
come together, the adroit weaving
in
and
out,
perfectly timed,

cows with painted horns strolling past
baskets of flowers and coconuts and *prasād*[3]
outside the temple, the long lines, the piles of shoes,
the bells clanging, people fervently whispering
into the ear of a statue,

the jostling of bodies pushing against each other,
the saris, the bright patterns of silk,
ornate curled-toe shoes,
medicine shops filled with Ayurvedic herbs,
jewelry stores gleaming with gold,
the swirl of it all
rolled, somehow,

1. *khus:* scent of vetiver
2. *mitti:* scent of earth and rain
3. *prasāda (prasād):* a sweet offered during a ceremony

into the scent of a single stick
of incense
carried back in a stuffed suitcase,
the hieroglyphic
of its spiral of scent
just
about
to
unfurl

Collective Ocean of Consciousness

Dear *Gaṅgā*,

From century upon century
of *pūjās*[1] and prayers,
entire temples washed
with sacred vibration,
the city sings,

light and love
streaming out into the chaotic streets,
into the hearts of those passing by,
washing into the collective ocean
of consciousness,
the merging of this
with that,

the rivers of our shared lives
crisscrossing as we flow
feeding into an unseen sea,
beyond our self-limitations
into the infinite freedom
of recognizing the other
within
the self

1. *pūjā:* Hindu religious ceremony

Feeding Upon the Light of Stars

Dear *Gaṅgā*,

Cartographers chart
  your length and width
    measuring
  through the years
your ever-changing self

and yet who can measure
    the mysticism of your flow,
  the ways you move,

      bursts of energy flowing
  in the mind or heart
    of someone who thinks of you,

    a voltage born of years
      of deep reflection,
    your waters feeding
      upon the light of the stars,
the luminous moon, the devotion
        of the sun,
            the iridescence
of the wings
    of large dragonflies
      as they pass

Unwinding Our Knots

Dear *Gaṅgā*,

The miracle of blooms,
bright orange,
on the tops of the trees

Fresh morning air, birdsong,
dogs barking, horns cheerful,
chanting from a temple,
calls to prayer at a nearby mosque,
the sounds of you
unfolding in the permutations
of vibrations of sound waves
unwinding our knots, carving
the shape of us slowly,
the way a waterfall reshapes the terrain,
the way waves redesign the shore

Your moisture inside the mouth's cave,
within rivulets of sweat,
streams of tears, everywhere
we are—you are, *jala,*[1]
with blessings,
with nourishment,
with cleansing,
with grace

1. *jala:* water

One Dissolving Particle at a Time

Dear *Gaṅgā*,

In the spirals and swirls of *mendhī*[1]
you are here, the graceful curved lines
of henna flowing
into interwoven flowers and designs
in a lineage of generations,
the beautiful art
of creative flow—

transformation of an arm or hand or foot
awakening in the bold thick dark design
on a canvas of flesh,
the slow drying of the paste
tightening upon the skin, the artwork
changing color and texture
to a smooth soft light brown design,

the impermanence coming and going—
the design of each day, each moment,
slowly, quickly fading
in the gradually fleeting nature of life—
the skin drying, shriveling, loosening,
casting off as the bones turn translucent
before transmuting to ash
before merging with your water,
elements receiving elements,
one dissolving
particle
at a time

---

1. *mendhī* (from *mendhikā*): the plant used in a form of temporary body art in India

Out of the Muddiest of Waters

Dear *Gaṅgā*,

In the quiet passageways
of sleep and the subconscious,
tributaries of *prāṇa*[1] flow

Glimmers of intuition, like light
upon your surface, an awareness
that comes and goes,
like clouds and clear sky alternating
in the changing weather of our mind,
our heart, the storms blowing through,
the languages of feeling
surpassing what the tongue can convey

Diverse rivers of words originating
from the same source, traveling
the expanse of understanding
and misunderstanding with equal grace
in the sea of *Hindī* or *Marāṭhī*[2] or *Gujarātī*,[3]
the universal expression of a smile
or frown
translating instantly,

1. *prāṇa:* life force
2. *Marāṭhī:* local language in *Mahārāṣṭra* region of India
3. *Gujarātī:* local language in Gujarat region of India

bypassing any complexity,
any barrier,
leaping
like a fish,
opalescent,
out of the muddiest
of waters

Your Abiding Waters

Dear *Gaṅgā,*

The confluence of loose ends,
earlier unknown pathways
all circling back to you
to this moment—
walking through a door
in a yoga studio with round walls
nestled in the palm trees of Pune[1]
and climbing, climbing . . .
steps leading to an overlook—

Beneath the head of a cobra,
Hanuman in red,
the faces of serpents all around,
the green and black wings of birds flocking by,
the rooftops, the treetops,
the absence of any other person,
the presence of all
who have traveled these steps before,
the sun, orange-tinged-gold,
glowing as it sets,
the teachings of a master
continuing years after his soul has released
from a body able to do all *āsanas,*[2]
the magnet of devotion
still strong, drawing thousands
from all over the world
to pay attention to thigh, shoulder, foot, hand,

1. Pune: city in India about four hours southeast of Mumbai (Bombay)
2. *āsana:* yoga pose

taking *Setu-bandhāsana*[1]
on the hard floor, taking *Ardha-candrāsana*[2]
hovering briefly in space,
taking *Śavāsana*[3] with a wooden block
resting on top of the stomach,
the breath lifting and lowering it gently,
the current of the life force
calmly rippling through
like your abiding waters

1. *Setu-bandhāsana:* Bridge pose in yoga
2. *Ardha-candrāsana:* Half-moon pose in yoga
3. *Śavāsana:* Corpse pose in yoga

Coming Together Like Two Hands in Prayer

Dear *Gaṅgā*,

In the flickering of the electricity and the Wi-Fi,
you flow. In the corridors of minds
flooded with fear, with sorrow, with delight,
with excitement, with worry, with devotion, with shame,
and in the throngs of people crowding
the outdoor market selling this and that
ghee lamps and garlands,
peacock feathers and *prasād*[1]
for 100 rupees, 200 rupees,
you rest like the sky, an awareness
without beginning or end, encompassing all that is—

the pain, the joy, the not knowing, the peace
born from believing in the universality,
the totality, the equal presence
of shadow
and light,
the merging
of yes and no
into simply being,
the resonance of silence
and sound,
the resistance and acceptance
coming together
like two hands in prayer,

the stillness of meditation

the calm point

1. *prasāda (prasād)*: a sweet offered during a ceremony

like the flame of the pyre, the pivotal point
of transcendence,
releasing earthly attachment,
opening to the expansiveness
the cosmic deliverance
of the limitless divine

That Space Within

Dear *Gaṅgā*,

The emotions come and go,
and do we, like you,
go with the flow,
or do we harden
like a rock?

Do we allow
the debris to flow past us,
or do we swallow it whole,
choking and
gasping?

Where is that distance,
that space within
to observe the drama
of the ego in all of its dances,
dramatic and bold
as they parade across
the mind's stage?

Watch the breath coming in,

watch the breath going out

Feel the breath flowing in,

feel the breath flowing out

Notice the upper body,
the lower body,

pay attention
  to the front of the body,
    the back of the body,

observing the left side of the body,
      the right side of the body,

breathing into every molecule
    of memory
circulating
            through

Beyond What Can Be Measured

Dear *Gaṅgā*,

You are the *iḍā*[1] and *piṅgalā*,[2]
the *suṣumṇā*,[3]
the life-giving rivers
of *prāṇa*[4] nourishing us,
your wisdom flowing
through us,
beyond what can be
measured or seen,
your currents of light
cascading over our hips,
shoulders, heels,
sacrum, sternum, skull,
the healing rivers of *prāṇa*
flowing through our lungs,
traveling our subtle energy pathways,
igniting the *prakāśa*[5] within—
the radiance, the splendor,
the effulgence, the brilliance,
the sun, moon, stars
reflecting,
glistening,
flickering,
glinting,
gleaming,
shimmering,

---

1. *iḍā:* lunar channel
2. *piṅgalā:* solar channel
3. *suṣumṇā:* central channel
4. *prāṇa:* life force
5. *prakāśa:* divine light

glittering
from your waters
in the confluence
coalescing in our consciousness
when we surrender,
go with the flow,
let go,
and breathe

Always Present, Always Flowing

Dear *Gaṅgā*,

You wait without waiting,
always present, always flowing,
always ready to receive whomever
and whatever shows up by your side

You are that ever-present awareness
constant in the midst of change,
the living example of acceptance,
santoṣa,[1] content with the vicissitudes,
observing the *līlā*,[2] the drama of life
unfolding as it will

the chants along your banks
washing over and again, the *śabda*[3]
of mantra purifying the rough borders
of anger, fear, greed, envy, grief—

japa[4] transmuting
and invigorating the air—
its molecules rejuvenating the lungs,
the *prāṇa*[5] circulating
throughout the body
irrigating the internal terrain
with new life, new light,
a river of *rasāyana*[6]
flowing within

---

1. *santoṣa:* referring to contentment; one of the *niyama* (guidelines for living) in yoga
2. *līlā:* divine play or dance
3. *śabda:* sound
4. *japa:* water
5. *prāṇa:* life force
6. *rasāyana:* rejuvenation therapy in *Āyurveda*

Accepting Every Leg, Every Arm

Dear *Gaṅgā*,

To which person, if any,
have you refused
your sacred healing waters?

What are the secrets
you will never tell?

What do you perceive
as you wash over
the bodies, both living
and dead?

You,
with your compassion,
accepting every leg, every arm,
every foot, every hand,
every heart heavy
with longing, with shame,
with sorrow, with regret—

to every mind
confused and searching
you bring your gentle flow
softening the sharp edges,
washing the particles of disbelief
in the midst of thick pollution
and the limitation of logic
in the midst of a world
consistently
persistently
racing
ahead

Until We Stop and Pause

Dear *Gaṅgā,*

The thick heat of stagnation
resting upon your waters,
rivers of sweat
pooling on the chests
of those strolling past you,
mosquitoes and dragonflies
skimming across your surface

Meanwhile, millions stuck
in traffic,
and zipping through tunnels
in subways,
flying through the air,
relaxing at home
reaching for the remote control,
sending text after text,
fixing meals, eating out,
running here and there,
oblivious to you

Knowing and not knowing
merging into a flow
of constant activity,
constant mind chatter,
until we stop and pause—

letting go of the need
to achieve,
to escape,
to be anywhere
other
than simply
here
inside the flow
of the
breath

Each Exhale Taking Us Closer

Dear *Gaṅgā*,

Along the riverbanks,
the *ghāṭs*,[1]
the gradual
reflections of faces,
tiny arroyos outlining
ancient eyes,
the etching of time
as it carries us
beyond comprehension
into an attachment
to this life,
believing the illusion
that this life, this world
is somehow our own,

the sun gilding your surface
for us the way it did
for those a hundred years ago,
a thousand years ago,

the wings of their lungs
expanding with each inhale
the way ours do now,

1. *ghāṭ* (from *ghaṭṭa*): steps leading down to a river

each exhale taking us closer slowly
to our last,
our lives a continual flowing . . .
even in the moments of stagnation
a momentum unseen, unfelt
carrying us
inevitably
forward

Resonance Eight Centuries Later

Dear *Gaṅgā,*

It's *Utpannā Ekādaśī,*
eleventh day after the new moon,
auspicious!
Thousands of pilgrims in the roads
walking to Alandi,
the men in all white—
the women in bright saris
carrying potted *tulsi*[1] plants
on their heads,
bowls with small mountains
of red and pink powders,
floods of people pouring in
from all directions—

Eight centuries later
devotion for Saint *Jñāneśvar*[2]
abundantly flowing
like the *Indrāyani* River
where marigolds lit with flame,
with prayers, float

Groups walking with flags,
dancing, singing,
making *raṅgoli*[3] designs
on the streets,
rivers of people
flowing into the temple,

---

1. *tulsi* (from *tulasī*)*:* holy basil herb
2. *Jñāneśvara:* a mystic *Marāṭhī* poet and yogi from the thirteenth century
3. *raṅgoli:* artistic designs made with colored sand, rice, or petals on special occasions

the long lines lengthening
rich with joy, with devotion,
bowed heads, offerings
of coconuts and *prasād,*[1]
the deities radiant,
resonant with rivers of sound
flowing from the lotus-hearts
of devotees
richly woven into chants
lifting up

1. *prasāda (prasād):* a sweet offered during a ceremony

You Are

Dear *Gaṅgā*,

You are the shine of sequins
glittering on the sari
on the shoulders of the woman
bending over to pick something up
on the side of the dirt road to *Jejuri*[1]
rough with gravel and potholes

You are the blessing of golden turmeric
flying through the air all around the temple
at the top of one hundred and sixty stone steps

You are the priest with the plate of petals
taking his finger with a *tilaka* to the forehead,
third eye, *ājñā cakra*[2] flowering, flowing,
the sounds of drums and tiny cymbals,
the garlands made of bright flowers,
large bowls of turmeric and *kumkum*,[3]
giant prayer bells,
the ghee lamps burning bright,
statues of deities with their eyes perpetually open
watching the progression

---

1. *Jejuri:* located in the Maharashtra *(Mahārāṣṭra)* region of India, home to *Khandoba* Temple
2. *ājñā cakra* (Ajna Chakra)*:* sixth chakra, located at the third eye
3 *kuṅkuma (kumkum):* red powder placed at the forehead ceremonially

of children,
goats,
dogs,
yogis,
beggars,
elders,
families,
and foreigners
here and there,

the entire cosmos
coming alive
atop this hill
tucked away
like a hidden
jewel

All of This and More

Dear *Gaṅgā*,

Wide bundles of fresh sugarcane
extending from opposite sides of a scooter
in a flock of scooters weaving along the backroad—

in traffic in Pune or Mumbai,
someone balancing
on the back of a scooter
casually texting, a family of four
on another scooter with two sleeping children
sandwiched between the parents,
scarves tied across faces covering noses and mouths
filtering out the pollution, the scarves
fluttering and flowing in the soft breeze
stirring the thick humid heat

You are all of this and more
with your encompassing,
continuing flow

Palms come together,
touching *tala hṛd*[1]
with *tala hṛd*,
fingertips pointing up
to the stars,

1. *tala hṛd:* a *marma* (acupressure) point in *Āyurveda* on the heart of the palm, calming to the mind and emotions

the sky full with the planets
    shifting and turning in their orbits,
  their patterns and designs a Jyotish[1] map
   of stelliums, *bhāvas,*[2] *daśās,*[3] *rāśis,*[4] *grahas*[5]
choreographing the time and location of each birth
    making possible even this moment now
  just as the fresh sugarcane from the fields
ultimately yields the nectar
    of fresh sugarcane juice

1. *Jyotiṣa:* Vedic astrology; in *Āyurveda,* the influence of the position of the planets at the time of one's birth is considered
2. *bhāvaḥ:* similar to a "house" in Western astrology
3. *daśā:* planetary period indicating which planets are ruling at specific times
4. *rāśi:* an individual's moon sign at the time of his or her birth
5. *graha:* planet

Universal Flow

Dear *Gaṅgā*,

Maladies of all forms—
shoulder pain, back pain,
skin disorders, high blood pressure,
hyperacidity, depression,
weight gain, weight loss,
anemia, anxiety
streaming into the clinics
one after another,

the rivers of suffering all flowing
toward the same sea
our compassion, our awareness, our humility,
awakening, gathering our vulnerabilities
one by one, bringing us face to face
with our mortality,
the impermanence—

māyā[1] convincing us
we are invincible
as if all who have gone before us
no longer exist in spirit form,

as if *yes* and *no* are two separate worlds,
as if the tangible and the intangible
are distinct,
different *lokas*,[2]

1. *māyā:* illusion
2. *loka:* world

as if the pathways of *prāṇa*[1]
and network of *nāḍīs*[2]
inside one person and the next
are not one and the same
like your ever-merging,
ever-changing
universal
flow

1. *prāṇa:* life force
2. *nāḍī:* subtle energy pathways in the body

The Singer and the Song

Dear *Gaṅgā,*

Is the river that receives one foot
the same river
that receives the other foot
in the ever-flowing current
of impermanence,
the illusions
dancing in dramas
the way rain dances upon a river
blurring the lines of where one starts
and the other ends

The call and response,
like a *kīrtan,*[1]
moving us in and out
and closer together,
the singer
and the song
merging together,
like night and day
sharing the same sky,

like *always* and *never*
inhabiting the same tongue,
like inhale and exhale
weaving through the same lungs,
like life and death
clothing
the very same
bones

1. *kīrtana (kīrtan):* a call and response music of praise in Sanskrit

Anchor of the Years

Dear *Gaṅgā*,

Your calm waters
a blessed reprieve
from the rough, sharp barbs,
your waters a balm
as you move with grace

With full awareness
of the depths of decay,
you continue to flow,
washing over any sharp piece of glass,
any foul debris,
inclusive of all,
exclusive of none, you accept
all the elements of this world:

the light
and the dark, the false
and the true,
the conflicted
and the pure

all of the rivers
of reality and illusion
present in you,
teacher, friend,
anchor of the years,
fearless guide
through
the ever-deepening
ever-mystifying
unknown

Breathing into the Space of Not Knowing

Dear *Gaṅgā,*

From so many different directions
    gratitude flows, like the mouths
        of many rivers
  opening out to the sea

  Gratitude for the *prāṇa*[1]
moving within the body
  nourishing us,
    flowing through the cells
in our plasma,
   circulating in our blood,
     awakening us

Can we appreciate the delay,
  the confusion,
     the discomfort
 as fully as we appreciate
   the laughter,
     the *laḍḍus,*[2]
 the embrace?

---

1. *prāṇa:* life force
2. *laḍḍu:* small round dessert from India

And what, if anything, is stopping us
from breathing courageously
into the space
of not knowing,
with spine elongated,
with heart open,
with mind as luminous
as the sun at dawn
rippling
your waters
awake?

Struggles Fading Away

Dear *Gaṅgā,*

You are the rivers of people
streaming into the temple[1]
in the middle of the city
to take *darśana*[2] of *Gaṇeśa,*[3]
one by one
offering coconuts
and bowing their heads,
amidst the abundance of fresh flowers
and sweet *prasād,*[4]
the smoke of *dhūp*[5] incense thickening
to the point the huge statue of *Gaṇeśa*
temporarily disappears

the flames of *ārati*[6] moving
in the large ghee lamps of the priests

zealous, fervent chanting:
males seated on one side,
females on the other,
drums and cymbals resounding,
the entire temple pulsating,
the light catching the colors
in the metallic designs on the walls,
an entire hour
of celebration

1. *Dagḍūśeṭh:* large temple to *Gaṇeśa* in Pune
2. *darśana:* beholding a deity or a revered person
3. *Gaṇeśa:* elephant-headed deity known for removing obstacles
4. *prasāda (prasād):* a sweet offered during a ceremony
5. *dhūpa:* a unique style of incense often used in sacred settings
6. *ārati (ārātrika, ārti):* ceremonial offering of light to a deity

The city outside
with its endless honking
and struggles
fading
away,
drivers pausing
in front of the temple,
pressing palms together
as they pass,
fingertips pointing up
to
the sky

River of Resonance

Dear *Gaṅgā*,

The sun rises here
with *Gāyatrī* mantra
on tongues
chanting to the light dawning,
the light glowing within,

the syllables of Sanskrit flowing
like you, river of redemption,
sunrise over your waters
synchronizing with sunset
across the world,

a vibration
of healing light
continuously flowing
in the offering of the *Gāyatrī*

Om bhūr bhuvaḥ svaḥ
tatsavitur vareṇyam[1]

River of resonance
transforming at the molecular level,
the fire, the earth, the water,
the space, the air all singing together
in harmony
the dance of life vibrating,
the music of the spheres
felt in the smallest of cells,
the light within glowing richly
as the sun's light gleaming
on your waters

1. *Om bhūr bhuvaḥ svaḥ tatsavitur vareṇyam:* the opening lines of the famous *Gāyatrī* mantra dedicated to the sun

Are We Not All a River

Dear *Gaṅgā*,

Are we not all a river
of mixing currents
and churning waters—

a river of pain,
a river of forgiveness,
a river of fury,
a river of sorrow,
a river of peace,
a river of fear,
a river of joy—

The river cloudy and clear,
or clear and cloudy,
depending upon what we trust
and what we fear

Oh *Gaṅgā*, deliver us
from our self-imposed
limitations,
open us to the river
without name
that flows
through us
all

Counterbalancing

Dear *Gaṅgā*,

Our breath flowing in and out,
cleansing us, purifying us, balancing us,
washing our ego, our anger, our sorrow,
our worry, our pride, our insecurity

Anuloma Viloma[1] balancing right and left side,
sun and moon,
anulom[2] and *pratilom*[3]
going with the current
and against the current,

counterbalancing this with that,
the ongoing choice of what to say,
what not to say,
what to do,
what not to do,
the coming and going
of our faith, our fear, our concentration,
our distraction, our devotion, our doubt,
as the tide ebbs and flows,

1. *Anuloma Viloma:* a balancing breath practice, also known as alternate nostril breath
2. *anulom:* going with the grain (in a natural flow)
3. *pratilom:* going against the grain

your presence, like *suṣumṇā*,[1] central channel,
lifeforce flowing,
the beauty of transformation
flourishing

You of purity, you of stagnation,
you of both/and
embracing, encompassing
the world as a whole,
its decay and disappointment
mixing in
with delight

1. *suṣumṇā:* central *nāḍī* (subtle energy pathway) running along the spine to the crown of the head

The Flow of Awareness

Dear *Gaṅgā*,

Within the flow
of awareness
no beginning
or ending,
all points
merging
into one

the start and the stop,
the known and unknown,
the resistance and surrender,
the rift and the reconciliation,
the collision
and the salvation,
the confusion and the compassion,
the burials and the births

the turbulence and the tranquility,
the relief and the despair,
the chaos and the calm,
the reticence and courage,
the resilience and fatigue,

the silence and sound,
moon and sun,
ocean and desert,
forest and field,
stars and sand,
breath and bones
Never and Always
harmonizing into resonance
like left palm
and right palm
joining together
at
heart center

You Bathe Us

Dear *Gaṅgā,*

In the *ślokas*[1] in the minds
of those who memorize
sacred scripture by heart,
you shimmer

In the *rāgas*[2] played on sitars
at certain times of day and night,
your waters shine

In the chants of those
waiting in line at the temples,
you dazzle

In the *sūtras*[3] flowing
in the minds
of students and scholars,
you glimmer

In the prayers offered
from open hearts,
you glow

In the silent music
of a circular design
of flowers floating in a bowl,
you delight

1. *śloka:* poetic verse in Sanskrit
2. *rāga:* a melody or pattern of notes in Indian classical music
3. *sūtra:* aphorism

In the deep silence
you bathe us
with acceptance,
resilience,

the movement
of your waters
creating a soft rhythm
in the sacred rivers
of night

Moving Beyond the Body

Dear *Gaṅgā*,

My soul remembers you
beyond the corridors
of mind's memory,

the resonance of sunrise
in *agnihotra*'s[1] flames,
the dance of fire,
the smell of camphor
at evening *ārati*,[2]
the pausing
for prayer,
the vibrations of sound
in the chants
flowing
like strands
of audible DNA,

the lineage
of generations of *Gāyatrī* mantra
transmitting bone to bone,
birth to birth,
its wisdom,
its intelligence
not extinguished
when the breath goes out,

1. *agnihotra:* ceremony to honor the sunrise and sunset
2. *ārati (ārātrika, ārti):* ceremonial offering of light to a deity

the spirit's pulse moving
beyond the body
like tiny boats of flowers with flame
moving away from shore,
the riverbank
receding
until only
current
remains

Reawakening

Dear *Gaṅgā,*

In the *rāgas*[1]
sung for thousands of years,
your palpable flow
alive in the dances
of fingers
upon the belly
of a drum,

the light of sun on water shimmering
in the chime of the small cymbals,
the dazzle of sun's brilliance
in the shake
of the tambourines,
the chants rippling
back
and forth
in call
and response,

the song of the soul illuminated
and illuminating
in the resonance
of the particles of sound
washing over us,
cascading through our heart and mind,

1. *rāga:* a melody or pattern of notes in Indian classical music

transformation at the cellular level
turning stagnation to salvation,
the mantras infusing directly
like intravenous fluid, revitalizing,
resuscitating us beyond the capacity
of anything tangible,

reawakening
our essence
into
light

Into the Sacred Spaces

Dear *Gaṅgā*,

In the village market,
giant cauliflower blossoms,
long carrots,
heaps of robust turmeric roots,
bitter melons, tiny eggplants,
sītāphala[1] sweet fruits,
large bags of rice and grains,
golden turmeric powder,

in the nearby temple
abhiṣek[2] of *śiva liṅgam*[3]
encircled by fresh blue flowers,

a train roaring past in the distance,
honking musics syncopating the air
as scooters, trucks, rickshaws, and small cars
weave in and out,
while in Alandi in the long lines
at the temple
people sing and chant
the names of *Tukārām* and *Jñāneśvar*,[4]
their poetry flowing across the centuries
into the present moment,

1. *sītāphala:* sugar-apple
2. *abhiṣeka:* a ritual of purification where liquid offerings like milk, ghee, and honey are poured over a *murti*
3. *śiva liṅgam:* a stone symbolic of Lord *Śiva*
4. *Tukārām:* seventeenth-century poet and saint from *Mahārāṣṭra;*
Jñāneśvara (Dnyaneshwar): thirteenth-century mystic poet and yogi from *Mahārāṣṭra*

the voices flowing like a timeless river
into the sacred spaces
where the saints
took *mahāsamādhi,*[1]
embracing the heavens,
dropping the body,
letting go of any attachment
to this earth

---

1. *mahāsamādhi:* a holy death, leaving the body consciously

Moving Beyond Language

Dear *Gaṅgā,*

In the stench,
in the rotting flowers
in soggy trash heaps
outside the temple,
you are here

In the fresh marigold and rose garlands
blessed by the temple priest
and now draped on the hood of our car
blessing the journey,
you are here

In the cold stares,
in the friendly smiles,
in the blending of English and *Hindī*
and *Marāṭhī,*[1]
you are here

In the jewelry shops
filled with gold chains and earrings,
with silver anklets,
and precious gems—
emerald, sapphire, ruby, and more,
you shine

In the patience of shopkeepers
dealing with foreigners,
your thousands-of-years presence
flows through

1. *Marāṭhī:* local language in *Mahārāṣṭra* region of India

Moving
beyond language,
we enter
your flow,
the purity
of the
wordlessness
of water
and air

With Each Breath

Dear *Gaṅgā*,

After thirty hours of winding through
the back roads of *Mahārāṣṭra*[1]
and threading through long lanes
leading into the temples of *Aṣṭa Vināyak*[2]
on *Gaṇapati Caturthī*,[3]
I am aboard a plane
in Chennai
and you are suddenly
just a few hours away

Long-imagined one,
your waters are becoming,
amazingly, almost within reach
as I find myself
inside the places on the map
I've gazed at for so long—

The cremation grounds of *Maṇikarṇikā*[4] call to me
in the way spirits rise up like mist,
their voices finding their way
through the subtlest spaces

---

1. *Mahārāṣṭra* (Maharashtra): a region of western India
2. *Aṣṭa Vināyaka:* a pilgrimage of visiting eight specific *Gaṇeśa* temples in the *Mahārāṣṭra* region in a particular order
3. *Gaṇapati Caturthī:* honoring *Gaṇeśa* on the fourth day of the waning moon cycle each month
4. *Maṇikarṇikā:* holy cremation ground on the riverbank of the *Gaṅgā*

The sky here in the upper atmosphere
  thousands of miles above India
is precisely the sky
    I have known faraway

 In the same way,
   you know each of us
dressed in our personalities,

  our bones
already beginning to fade—

 the humerus,
  the ulna,
the cheekbone,
  the scapula
slowly
  becoming
   more
translucent
     with
  each
    outgoing
 breath

Thousands of Years of Prayers

Dear *Gaṅgā*,

At sunset *ārati*,[1]
anchored boats shift
in your dark waters,
the synchronized movements
of the priests
mesmerizing the crowd
as they chant and lift their ghee lamps,
tossing flower petals,
honoring the sun's journey,
circling fans of peacock feathers—
larger versions of the ones sold by young boys
on the streets of Pune near *Dagḍūśeṭh*[2] temple—

their symmetry, their feathery iridescence
resonating, their reappearance in *ārati*
by your side at dusk
startling like the cobra rising up
from a lidded basket
in front of a man in bright clothes
appearing to be a *sādhu*[3]

---

1. *ārati (ārātrika, ārti):* ceremonial offering of light to a deity
2. *Dagḍūśeṭh:* a large temple to *Gaṇeśa* in Pune
3. *sādhu:* holy person

In the reflection of candles floating
in small baskets filled with fresh flowers
a silent song made of generations of offerings
sings its way through light and water,
thousands of years of prayers
at sunset and sunrise
transmuting the mist
into
song

Undeniable *Saṃskāras*

Dear *Gaṅgā*,

Pilgrims
arrive on foot
carrying belongings
on their heads
singing *bhajans*[1]
accompanied by *tabla*[2]
and cymbals
deep into the night
while garbage floats
on your surface—
undeniable *saṃskāras*,[3]
dichotomies
swimming outside of logic,
bacteriophages
re-oxygenating your waters,
as sewage infuses into you,

and are we not all part of this,
worries, regrets, judgments
polluting the channels
of our mind—
the 72,000 *nāḍīs*
throughout our body
clogging with unresolved emotions
our immune systems
staggered
by the sheer influx
of toxic thoughts,

---

1. *bhajan* (from *bhajana*): devotional song
2. *tabla:* a pair of hand drums used in Indian music
3. *saṃskāra:* mental impression or pattern

the sacred portals
of our ears and eyes
taxed by sights and sounds
of a world turning in on itself—

May we, with grace,
pause to slow down,
to observe the flow
of shadow and light,
to look within,
to give thanks,
to renew

In the midst
of these swirling currents,
pausing,
with grace,
may we slow down,
observing the flow
of shadow and light
in us and around us,
looking softly
with awareness
and compassion,
accepting the intermingling
of day and night
within us all

In the Quiet Knocking of Boats

Dear *Gaṅgā*,

Your legendary presence dwarfs us
in the way worries become small
in the vast fields of cornstalks
swaying in the sun,

in the heaps of sugarcane pulled from the fields
turning to juice amidst the shaking bells
of a sugarcane machine,
in the hundreds of goats
being herded by the side of the road,

in the lilting rhythms
of the *stotras*[1] and *bhajans*[2]
at the temples,
in the bright colors and patterns
of the saris
billowing in the thick air,
in the mysterious ways
of time and space unfolding,

in the miracle of a lost passport being found
at the airport in Chennai,
in the question of a Swedish woman on the plane asking,
"Where are the women along the *ghāṭs*[3]?"

in the voice of a French woman at the Varanasi airport
describing how much the city has changed in thirty years,

1. *stotra:* hymn of praise
2. *bhajan* (from *bhajana*)*:* devotional song
3. *ghāṭ* (from *ghaṭṭa*): steps leading down to a river

in the quiet knocking of boats against each other
in the early morning breeze,

in the worn feet of an eighty-year-old rickshaw driver
pedaling through the crowded streets,

in the moment
when I must turn away
from you
and move back
into
the
world

To the Heavens

Dear *Gaṅgā,*

I have come and gone,
and you remain

Today, someone new is strolling beside you,
peering into your depths
where the vestiges of holy men rest
in the mouths of fish

The area from the bridge to *Asi Ghāṭ*[1]
a tapestry of *ghāṭs,*[2] children, boats, dogs, goats

Mā Gaṅgā[3]
and the *makara*[4] she rides upon
keeping watch from her temple
at *Daśāśvamedh Ghāṭ*[5]

Each day, with your grace,
sometimes two hundred
exquisite skeletons set aflame—

the bodies of children, pregnant women, lepers,
holy men, and those dying by cobra bite
tied to a stone for you to swallow...

---

1. *Asi Ghāṭ:* the southernmost *ghāṭ* in Varanasi
2. *ghāṭ* (from *ghaṭṭa*): steps leading down to a river
3. *Mā Gaṅgā:* the goddess of the Ganges, reverential name for River *Gaṅgā*
4. *makara:* divine crocodile-like being
5. *Daśāśwamedh Ghāṭ:* the largest and liveliest *ghāṭ* in Varanasi

The eternal fire of *Śiva* burning
for thousands of years
in the heart
of the cremation grounds,
smoke rising—

the bundles of long-dried grasses carrying this torch
into each new body as its soul begins its journey
up the invisible stairs from the *ghāṭs* to the heavens

the monkeys on the rooftops with their acrobatics,
some pseudo holy men posing for photos with tourists,
cellphone cameras trying to capture
the ancient sunrise ceremonies
and the illumination
of your waters
in the orange light

Carrying Away Fear

Dear *Gaṅgā,*

In an Ayurvedic healing village[1] in southern India,
a worn book[2] appears
in an outdoor library open one hour a day,
your 108 names
pouring forth
in an unexpected tributary:

"*Nata-bhiti-hrt* carrying away fear
Nayananda-dayini affording delight to the eye
Srimati auspicious
Amrtakara-salila whose water is a mine of nectar
Sankha-dun-dubhi-nisvana making a noise like a conch
shell and drum
Sighra-ga swift-flowing
Siddha perfect, holy
Saranya yielding help, shelter, protection
Saphari-purna full of fish
Satya-sandha-priya dear to the faithful
Ananta eternal
Om-kara-rupini having the appearance of the sacred
syllable Om
Svarga-sopana-sarani staircase to Heaven
Santi-santana-karini bringing about the continuance
of peace
Samsara-visa-nasini destroying the power of illusion
Sarangata-dinarta-paritrana protector of the sick and
suffering who come to you for refuge

---

1. *Vaidyagrāma*
2. *Slowly Down the Ganges* by Eric Newby

Samukti-da giving complete spiritual emancipation
Puratana ancient
Punya auspicious
Ajnana-timira-bhanu a light amid the darkness of ignorance"[1]

These names finding me, flowing
through my veins,
through the tributaries of my mind
as I remember how ordinary you appeared
beside the cremation grounds,
so humble
as if you were any other river,
nondescript

1. Names excerpted from "The 108 Names of the Ganges" included in *Slowly Down the Ganges* by Eric Newby, pp. 6–11

Sacred Bridge

Dear *Gaṅgā*,

At a small temple to *Dhanvantari*[1]
in southern India,
the birds watch
as a young priest's chants flow
into a conversation
of chants
flowing
back
and forth,
in Sanskrit,
our sacred bridge

The always-open eyes of *Dhanvantari* look on,
the ghee lamps flicker,
the reddish-pink flowers
of the fresh garland bright
against the dark stone of the deity

Another young priest arriving with a *dholak*[2]
begins to play—the music awakening
the night into a thousand stars—
moments spilling into each other
until hours have passed

1. *Dhanvantari:* unparalleled physician in *Āyurveda*
2. *dholak:* an oblong drum strapped to the body

and I drift, as if in a dream,
back to my mosquito-netted bed
where the *auṣadha*[1] of *śabda*[2]
continues to flow,
irrigating
each and every one of my veins
with devotion
and delight

1. *auṣadha:* medicine
2. *śabda:* sound

Beckoning Me to Stay

Dear *Gaṅgā*,

How did you see me
confused at the entrance
of *Eachanari Vinayagar*[1] temple
near *Coimbatore*
not knowing which way to go,
nearly forgetting to remove my sandals,
the five flights awaiting me
scattering my mind . . .

A voice says, "You can come with us"
and suddenly: the sanctum sanctorum,
priests giving blessings to us in *Tamil*,
Gaṇeśa himself only a few steps away...

You flow in the thick banana-jaggery mix
of *prasād* poured into my hand
You flow in my tears as the grandma
invites me to her home

They do not know I am on my way
to the airport, the driver Ganesh
waiting for me outside

You flow in the breeze
swaying the trees,
the lush green of the countryside
beckoning me to stay
even as the wheels of the Ganesh-driven car
roll ever closer to *Peelamedu*[2]

1. *Eachanari Vinayagar* temple: temple to *Gaṇeśa* near *Coimbatore* in *Tamil Nāḍu*
2. *Peelamedu:* location of *Coimbatore* International Airport

Into Your Waters

Dear *Gaṅgā*,

Do you remember me,
the way my eyes followed
the wrapped bodies
being carried by family members,

the men carrying the bodies
down into your waters
cleansing them for their journey,
placing them on the metal forms

to be lit by a torch
from *Śiva*'s eternal fire
burning hundreds of bodies a day
for thousands of years,

the skull bursting open with a pop,
the soul dropping its body
like an old coat,
the family members
encircling the body

some taking photos on their phones,
or sending texts, some staring
with blank faces, others watching
the bystanders watching them,

all joining with the onlookers
of cows,
goats wearing shirts,
and hungry wild-eyed dogs
keen to the scent
of burning
flesh

Nourished by Your Waters

Dear *Gaṅgā*,

I think of you as I wait
to board the plane in Coimbatore,
currents of sweet memories
flooding my heart as I travel north to Mumbai,
the spicy fire of the airline *poha*[1]
igniting my tongue

Across the wild highways of Mumbai
in a tiny car with luggage on the roof,
a perilous, miraculous flow to the next terminal
in a fog-driven delay,
and I remember you—

the early morning boat ride across your waters,
the young boy Sunil paddling the oars through the cold fog
toward *Asi Ghāṭ* for sunrise *ārati*—

In the cold airport at night,
people from distant parts of the world
Face-Timing in unknown languages,
all of us flowing to destinations
disparate and the same—

The river of night deepens, Delhi
catapulting into an international flight, nearly missed,
the *vibhūti*[2] from the *Eachanari* temple
in a tiny envelope in my purse,

1. *poha:* Indian dish of cooked rice flakes
2. *vibhūti:* sacred ash

each minute taking me further away from you,
from the pulsation of a life, a world nourished by your waters

At Newark, luggages circulating for hours at baggage claim
in the predawn hours of morning, one delay
cascading into another, flight to Denver nearly missed,
luggage lost by Denver...

One more flight,
and my body drifts home
the way bodies find their way to you
at the completion
of a long-awaited journey...
the next one,
without instructions,
already begun—

Beyond Reach

Dear *Gaṅgā*,

Returned to the desert
like a misdelivered package,
I show up in the bleakness of winter chill,
bare feet replaced with warm socks
and close-toed shoes,
short sleeves and sun-warmed skin buried
in winter coat,
wool scarf,
gloves,
and a hat

I wake up in odd hours of the night
unsure of where I am,

body-clock resetting slowly,
body here,
mind and soul still traveling…

I look for any semblance of you,
any droplet of your grace

"How was your time in India?"
and words begin to spill from my lips,
words that make little sense, even to me
who walked miles by your side for hours,
who sat beside you
as the priests lit the camphor
to light the flames to honor you
at the setting of the sun,

at the rising of the sun,
to sweep the peacock feathers
in circular motion,

to toss flower petals into the air,
to chant the mantras
blessing you at the *sandhi*[1]
of night and day,
the mystery of your essence
always
just beyond
reach

1. *sandhi:* juncture, joint, point of transition

Appearing Like Magic

Dear *Gaṅgā*,

Early one morning
through the thick haze
of the first months
of the pandemic,
you call,
finding a way
across time and space,
a videocall on WhatsApp
connecting us:
the sunset *ārati*[1] festivities
scaled down to one priest,
the large crowd reduced
to a handful of helpers,
the thick traffic of boats absent—

the *darśana*[2] of the priest
in the one moment
he turns toward the camera
like a burst of light,
the scent of the incense
filling my nostrils
many thousands of miles away,
the healing waters of you
flowing in my tears of joy

you, appearing like magic,
just when needed,

1. *ārati (ārātrika, ārti):* ceremonial offering of light to a deity
2. *darśana:* beholding a deity or a revered person

spirit bogged down
by one too many losses,
yet even the thousands of deaths
not unfamiliar to you
with the daily company you keep
of souls setting flight,
leaping up the invisible stairway
to the next *loka,*[1]
leaving the no-longer-needed bones
behind

1. *loka:* world

Our Invincibility Dissolving

Dear *Gaṅgā*,

Tributaries of thoughts
and emotions surging
amidst the prayers and hopes,
a steady stream
of anticipations, frustrations,
competitions, expectations,
jails filled to overflowing,
minds imprisoned
in fear, doubt, despair,
hospitals teeming
with gunshot wounds,
pandemic distress, heart attacks,
cancers spreading

A thought of you
washing the pain
with peace,
even if just for a moment—
your open-eyed remembrance
through millennia of suffering,
steadfast witness
to *this* pain, *this* prayer,

our invincibility
dissolving,
all of our
possessions
and ambitions
dissolving,
our entire life
dissolving
into
one mere drop
in the continuous
ever-abiding
flow

By Your Waters

Dear *Gaṅgā*,

How many yogis have sat
in *Padmāsana*[1] by your waters,
their legs folded like a lotus,
their mantra-rich minds
purifying the *āma*[2]
in mind-body and the atmosphere

How many yogis have sat
by your waters in predawn,
steeping in the nectar
of *brāhmamuhūrta*[3]
practicing *prāṇāyāma*[4]
cleansing the *nāḍīs*,[5]
the thousands
of subtle rivers
circulating within,

and how many yogis
have gathered
near *Asi Ghāṭ*
after sunrise *ārati*[6]
to practice *āsana*,[7]

1. *Padmāsana:* Lotus pose in yoga
2. *āma:* Ayurvedic term for toxic waste
3. *brāhmamuhūrta:* sacred time before dawn, ideal for spiritual practice
4. *prāṇāyāma:* one of the eight limbs of yoga; devoted to breathwork
5. *nāḍī:* subtle energy pathways in the body
6. *ārati (ārātrika, ārti):* ceremonial offering of light to a deity
7. *āsana:* yoga pose

hundreds
at a time
taking *Baddha Koṇāsana,*[1]
rising to Warrior I
before moving into the flow
of *Sūrya Namaskār,*[2]
their bodies warming,
their cells shining,
the luminosity of the sun
weaving itself
into the very elements
of their being

1. *Baddha Koṇāsana:* Bound Angle pose in yoga
2. *Sūrya Namaskār:* Sun salutation

Lifesong

Dear *Gaṅgā,*

What do you hear
from the *navagraha,*[1]
as they hold *satsaṅg*[2] with you
flowing within
the endless devotion
of the sky?

Do they tell you
stories of the birth
of the constellations,
the geometry of their light
in ongoing meditation
blessing the night's frequencies
as moonlight mesmerizes
the monkeys?

Jyotiṣīs[3] in the mazes
of Benares[4] offering maps
of the future
to tourists

1. *navagraha:* nine planets
2. *satsaṅga:* a gathering for spiritual purpose
3. *Jyotiṣī (Jyotiṣika):* astrologer trained in Vedic astrology
4. Benares: another name for the city of Varanasi *(Vārāṇasī)*, also called Kashi *(Kāśī)*

And what, dear *Gaṅgā*,
is your rising sign? Which planets
inhabit your fourth house?
What is the precise day and time
of your birth?

Within which holy moment
did your first droplets appear
with only the quietest hint
of the lifesong
they would become?

Storm-Laden Lungs

Dear *Gaṅgā,*

Even when those
in the next town,
or next door,
are unreachable,

you are there
running through us,
there as you have been
for the lepers,
those having no rupees,[1]

those whose only friends
are the fish,
the sky,
and the moon,

those keeping watch
for the boat
that never returns,

those keeping a cobra
rising to the song
of a flute,

those bearing
storm-laden lungs
thick with the loss
of a loved one,
the body
preparing
to burn

1. rupee *(rūpya):* Indian unit of money

Like a Boat Not Yet Seen

Dear *Gaṅgā*,

How many winters
have you seen pass,
the icy winds huddling people
deeper into scarves and shawls
as they cross your waters
under thick gray skies?

The fingers of the priests
warming with the ghee lamps
they hold predawn
before a sliver of sunlight
has pierced the sky

Your sacred waters
traveling from the *Himālayas*
to *Prayāg*,[1]

devotees visiting you there,
shaking off winter
in the sweet embrace
of *Vasant Pañcamī*,[2]

the promise of spring
in forty days
floating in the distance
like a boat not yet seen,

the horizon still without a hint
of anything beyond
the limitless bleak black cold

1. *Prayāg:* also known as *Prayāgraj* and *Allahabad, or Ilāhābād*
2. *Vasanta Pañcamī:* a festival marking the beginning of spring

An Inexplicable Resonance

Dear *Gaṅgā*,

How often do you receive
the ashes or bones
of those you've received before,
their recycled lives
fooling them,
but not you?

Do you recognize by feel
their four or five incarnations,
their patellas
and clavicles
woven
into renewed skeletal structures,
different genders,
distinctive facial features
presenting new faces to the world?

The soul, housed inside
the bones and flesh,
remembering
without remembering
a previous life

only in brief moments
shrugged aside—

a glimmer,
a sense of *déjà vu*
an inexplicable resonance
like a *mantra* appearing
in the mouth
of the mind
from some
unidentified source

Blooming Unseen

Dear *Gaṅgā*,

When we chant
Devi sureśvari
bhagavati Gaṅge[1]
all the way across
the world,
how much
of the resonance
do you feel,

the light particles
of sound
moving quickly
in a transmission
bypassing time and space

Within the molecules
of your waters,
ancient symmetrical
metaphysical shapes
blooming unseen,

your blessings upon us
abundant,
generously flowing

1. *Devi sureśvari bhagavati Gaṅge:* opening lines of the famous *Gaṅgā Stotram*

even as we hold
in our mouths
the sacred syllables

Bhāgīrathi sukha dāyini mātas
tava jala mahimā nigame khyātaḥ[1]

Thousands of years
of praise
and mercy
echoing
in the duet
between
your sacred song
and our very human
tongues

1. *Bhāgīrath sukha dāyini mātas tava jala mahimā nigame khyātaḥ* : part of *Gaṅgā Stotram*

Awakening the Stars

Dear *Gaṅgā*,

It is early morning
in the desert,
the pandemic,
more than
a year later,
still turning us
inside out

With devotion,
one priest
still offers
ārati[1] to you
at the *sandhi*[2]
of every sunrise
and sunset

In an orange shirt
with a sash,
he holds the bell
in his hand
awakening the stars

His other hand
circling incense—
a large ghee lamp
shaped like a small pine tree
illuminating the night,

1. *ārati (ārātrika, ārti):* ceremonial offering of light to a deity
2. *sandhi:* juncture, joint, point of transition

puddles of rainwater
glistening in the light

A cracked-open coconut,
a shower of rose petals,
a cobra lamp,
sacred hair of cow tails,
fans of peacock feathers,
the statue of *Mā Gaṅgā*,

and in the background
of the small rectangular window
of my phone connecting us
across thousands of miles,
policemen patrol,
enforcing the quarantine curfew
as you, dear *Gaṅgā*,
continue your flow,
uninterrupted

When Your Waters Braid

Dear *Gaṅgā,*

When your waters braid,
do you hear
the silent songs
of *Sarasvatī*[1]
as she swims beneath,
far from view,

do you share with *Yamunā*[2]
how the nearly dissolved particles
of the charred bodies
cry out to you
aching for resolution,
for absolution,

the *ātma*[3] separating
from the *śarīra,*[4]
the body and soul
going their separate ways,

your waters tuned
to hear
the voice of each,

---

1. *Sarasvatī:* a holy mystic river in India said to braid with the rivers *Gaṅgā* and *Yamunā*
2. *Yamunā:* a major tributary of River *Gaṅgā*
3. *ātman:* soul
4. *śarīra:* body

their holographic sounds
converted
to nearly undefinable
colors, glimmerings of light,
patterns that are not patterns
but molecular movements
ancient as what's buried
in your riverbed, sifting
with the silt
and the sand

Flowing Like a Chant Without End

Dear *Gaṅgā*,

How cold you are
at your source,
how pure
your waters
dripping like ambrosia
from the glaciers
in the *Himālayas*,

the most dedicated
of devotees trekking
to visit with you
at *Gaṅgotrī*,[1]

thousands tracing
and retracing
the pilgrimage,

the footsteps
of the centuries
layered
with new footprints,
mobile phones
and digital cameras
now packed
in the pockets
of those
trying to capture
something
of your glory,

1. *Gaṅgotrī:* a sacred location, considered to be one of the origins of the River *Gaṅgā*

the rush
  of your rich song

your waters flowing
  like a chant without end,
    a *japa*[1] of *jala*[2]
  celestially pure

1. *japa:* repetition of a mantra
2. *jala:* water

A Million Tiny Circles Expanding

Dear *Gaṅgā*,

Monsoon season
 the late afternoon storms
  building,
 thickening,
  darkening,

the sky breaking open
 over you,
  the rainwaters
 falling into you,
  into a million
 tiny
circles
 expanding

the thunder rumbling
 in the reunion,
  the visitation of waters
 from the heavens,
messengers of *Gaṅgā Mā*[1]
 dancing with invisible
  silver anklets, their bells
 making music audible
only to the fish—

Your blessings
 flowing
  far
 and
  wide

---

1. *Gaṅgā Mā:* the goddess of the *Ganges*, reverential name for River *Gaṅgā*

Wellsprings of Peace

Dear *Gaṅgā*,

What do you feel
as researchers
scoop your waters
into vials,
as they study
your molecules
and spin
your particles,
high-power microscopes
peering into you,

your essence
beyond what is
easily measured,
logged,
documented,
or catalogued,
the rapidity
of your re-oxygenation
boggling scientific minds,

the muscle and magic
of your bacteriophages
eating through
the debris
at record pace
creating
within
the pollution
sacred
wellsprings
of peace

Your Holy *Jal*

Dear *Gaṅgā*,

How humble you are
flowing so many miles
for millennia nonchalantly
when it is you, your holy *jal*[1]
carried to temples near and far
by countless devotees
for thousands of years

when it is you, your holy *jal*
awakening thousands, millions
so early to bathe in your waters,
with prayers to cleanse
the body, the mind, the heart

when it was you, your holy *jal*,
your purifying power
turning poison, *Kālakūṭa*,
into *amṛt*,
the nectar of immortality[2]

miracle and malady
light and shadow
intertwining
even now
as trash floats
on the surface
of your
divine
waters

1. *jal (jala):* water
2. Reference to the story of *Samudra Manthana* (the churning of the ocean) in Indian culture

The Music of the Full Moon

Dear *Gaṅgā,*

The music of the full moon
shimmering in your dark waters
like sparkling jewels,
devotees preparing to take a bath
in your waters during moonrise,
offering prayers

How many full moons have shone
upon your waters?

How many new moons
have come and gone,
the lunar cycle shifting gradually
from crescent to full moon
its sparkling celestial light
illuminating your flow

The purification of your waters
irrigating the channels
of the mind
with
light

Not the First Time

Dear *Gaṅgā*,

Images of dead bodies
  floating in you
surfacing continents away,
    the pandemic and its suffering
gone viral too quickly
  to measure—
volunteers at temples
    in makeshift clinics
offering oxygen—

Yet this is not the first time
  you have held softly
    bodies ravaged—
  cyclical plagues
through the ages
  you witness
    always
      with steadfast
   grace

A friend
and her grandma
  hospitalized in *Mahārāṣṭra*[1]
      with Covid
now released—
  small miracles
      amidst the devastation
  like small candles floating
through thousands of nights

1. *Mahārāṣṭra* (Maharashtra): located in western India; the second-most populous state in India

Tīrtha

Dear *Gaṅgā*,

Beneath a small wooden bridge
in the woods in the winter,
a stream rippling over rocks
catches the light,
the sun brilliant
on its waters, shining like a jewel,
the ephemeral luminosity
of this *tīrtha*[1] sacred
as the flow of your spirit
through *Kāśī*,[2]
the way
you reappear
when least expected
in droplets of a shower, a bath,
in the *jyoti*[3] illuminating
someone's eyes, radiant,
in the side-by-side
of devastation and divine,
of chaos and calm,
in the momentary crossing
of yes and no,
then and now—
tiny portals
tunneling through
time
and
space

---

1. *tīrtha:* a sacred crossing
2. *Kāśī:* Kashi, "City of Light," another name for Varanasi and Benares
3. *jyoti:* divine light

Sacred Moon

Dear *Gāṅga,*

I awaken before dawn
  in the cold of autumn,
all of the tall trees having let go
  of their leaves, surrendering

New variants of the virus
  circulating but not yet
making themselves known

Invited for *Dev Dīvali,*[1] I wait
  for the moment when the river
of Wi-Fi will connect us...

Through the weak signal,
  the chants and singing
flow in and out, the images
  blur, but for two full minutes
during the two-hour ceremony,
  the connection is crystal clear,
and through my phone,
  I can see all the tiny lights
outlining you, and the lights
  shining from the boats passing by

Meanwhile, on my laptop,
  a livestream from Rishikesh
broadcasts images
  of a simultaneous *ārati,*

1. *Dev Dīvali:* festival of lights at full moon *(Pūrṇimā)* in the month of *Kārtika*

multiplying the flow
of chanting
and ghee lamps honoring you

All the ceremonies
of light beneath the luminous sacred moon
sending reverberations of reverence
through your waters...the blessings flowing
all the way across the world,
the light reflecting from you
and from the faces
of those chanting by your side with love
awakening us,
yet again,
to miracle

Your Deep Knowing

Dear *Gaṅgā*,

In our two-footedness
we stumble,
our best intentions
careening into each other,
our egos unplacated by the roar
of mortality unheard in the spin
of unseeable forces torqueing us
in infinite directions

Meanwhile, you carry on
in an unbroken *japa*,[1]
your *jala*[2]
silently repeating
the sound
of all that is sacred

your ancient waters
so much wiser
than all of our learning,
the rapidity
of our interconnectivity
no match for your depth,
for your deep knowing
of the earth,
the way you glide upon it,

1. *japa:* repetition of a mantra
2. *jala:* water

how devotedly
you carry the ashes
of lives pulverized
by death's
inevitable
flash

The Journey of This Book

Going to India was something I dreamt of even as a child. It's one of those dreams that I couldn't explain, though I felt it rooted deep in my heart. This dream came into sharper focus as I encountered yoga and *Āyurveda* as an adult. When the stars finally aligned for me to go to India, I was thrilled. However, even with all the videos I watched, articles I read, and conversations I had with those who had traveled to India, my mind was not at peace. As the departure date came closer and closer, it just felt overwhelming to me to fly across the world to India on my own. Around this time, the idea floated into my mind one day to write a letter to the *Gaṅgā* River. The desire to visit this sacred river when I went to India was very much in my heart, so much so, in fact, that I ended up, once again, making a journey on my own—this time from Pune to Varanasi to visit River *Gaṅgā*.

After I wrote the first letter to the *Gaṅgā* River—in the form of a poem—I felt so much better, and I began writing a poem-letter to River *Gaṅgā* each day. This continued during my two months in India and then occasionally after I returned at the end of 2019. Once the pandemic began, I didn't write much creatively; however, about a year into the pandemic, I began to look back at my poems and realized they had become a book. When Shanti Arts accepted the poetry collection for publication, editing continued. It has been a complete delight to work with Christine Cote at Shanti Arts, and I am grateful for the entire journey that continues even now as I share these poems with you, dear readers.

Gratitude

I express my deep appreciation . . .

. . . to the friends I met in India—Aili, Ashinth, Bernard, Darshan, Farook, Hemangi, Kajsa, Machindra, Nitin, Prashant, Priyanka, Puja, Purnima, Rajendra, Santosh, Somit, Vicky, Vimal, the team at *Vaidyagrāma*, and the entire VIOA group;

. . . to those who helped me prepare for India—Annie, Ashley, Aunt Sara-Ellen, Binita, Cory, Eileen, Gigi, Gloria, Howard, Jeanne, Joan, Jill, Kathy, Kirsten, Mariam, Patrick, Petra, Rinita, Rosanne, Sarah, Shannon, Sonal, Sonya, Surinder, and Uncle Eddie;

. . . to all the kind strangers whose names I do not know who, like angels, helped me at just the right times along my journey in India;

. . . to those who lovingly read my poems in various drafts;

. . . to all of my teachers of poetry, Sanskrit, yoga, and *Āyurveda;*

. . . to you, dear readers, for sharing this journey with me;

. . . to Dr. Vasant Lad for creating The Ayurvedic Institute in Albuquerque along with Vasanta Institute of Ayurveda (VIOA) near Pune, and for inspiring me with his knowledge, wisdom, creativity, kindness, and wonderful stories of India;

. . . to my parents, Karen and Jim Dunlop, for supporting my life's journey with love;

. . . and, of course, to the beauty, wisdom, and grace of India and River *Gaṅgā*.

Julie Dunlop is a poet, an author, and a teacher of yoga, *Āyurveda*, and writing. Her book *Ocean of Yoga: Meditations on Yoga and Āyurveda for Balance, Awareness, and Wellbeing*, was published by Singing Dragon in London in 2017 and offers a mixture of prose and poetry. Her second book, *Honoring the Light in You* (Finishing Line Press, 2022) is a collection of poems sharing stories of yoga in daily life. Dunlop's previous chapbook publications include *Breath, Bone, Earth, Sky* (2014) and *Bending Back the Night* (2012). Her poetry has been published in many national journals, including the *Journal of the American Medical Association* (*JAMA*), *The Threepenny Review, Poet Lore, North Carolina Literary Review, South Dakota Review, Atlanta Review, Cold Mountain Review,* and *Appalachian Heritage*. Additionally, her prose has appeared in the *Ayurveda Journal of Health, Radiologic Technology, JAMA, Appalachian Heritage,* and *Wake Forest Magazine*. Dunlop has taught daily yoga classes in the weeklong wellbeing program (*Pañcakarma*) at the Ayurvedic Institute in Albuquerque, New Mexico for five years, and she enjoys sharing pathways to wellbeing with the community through classes and workshops; she is certified through Yoga Alliance as a yoga teacher (RYT 500 + E-RYT 200) and through the National Ayurvedic Medical Association as an Ayurvedic Practitioner (CAP). In 2019, she traveled to India to experience the birthplace of yoga and *Āyurveda* and to deepen her studies of *Āyurveda* at Vasanta Institute of Ayurveda (VIOA). She also holds a BA in English from Wake Forest University and an MA in English from the University of New Mexico. With gratitude, she integrates the ancient wisdom of yoga and *Āyurveda* into her writing, supporting the harmony of body, mind, and spirit at the heart of wellbeing.

www.ingramcontent.com/pod-product-compliance
Lightning Source LLC
Chambersburg PA
CBHW042134160426
43199CB00022B/2913
* 9 7 8 1 9 5 6 0 5 6 6 8 6 *